John Todhunter

A Sicilian Idyll

A Pastoral Play in Two Scenes

John Todhunter

A Sicilian Idyll
A Pastoral Play in Two Scenes

ISBN/EAN: 9783337865139

Printed in Europe, USA, Canada, Australia, Japan

Cover: Foto ©Thomas Meinert / pixelio.de

More available books at **www.hansebooks.com**

A SICILIAN IDYLL.

A SICILIAN IDYLL

A Pastoral Play

IN TWO SCENES

BY

JOHN TODHUNTER

Δεῦτέ νυν, ἄβραι Χάριτες, καλλίκομοί τε Μοῖσαι.—SAPPHO.

LONDON
ELKIN MATHEWS
AT THE SIGN OF THE BODLEY HEAD
IN VIGO STREET
1890

A SICILIAN IDYLL
BY JOHN TODHVNTER

TO

FLORENCE EMERY.

DRAMATIS PERSONÆ.

Amaryllis; } Shepherdesses.
Thestylis; }

Alcander ; a Mountain Shepherd.

Daphnis; a Shepherd of the Vales.

First Shepherd.

Second Shepherd.

Attendant on Amaryllis.

Chorus of Shepherds and Shepherdesses.

Three days are supposed to elapse between the first and second scenes.

B

ORIGINAL CAST.

AMARYLLIS	MISS FLORENCE FARR.
	(MRS. EDW. EMERY.)
THESTYLIS	MISS LILY LINFIELD.
	(MRS. A. L. BALDRY.)
ALCANDER	MR. H. M. PAGET.
DAPHNIS	MR. E. HERON ALLEN.
FIRST SHEPHERD	MR. MOWBRAY MARRAS.
SECOND SHEPHERD	MR. W. HERBERT ROE.
ATTENDANT	MISS CHRISTINE CONNELL.

THE PROLOGUE spoken by MR. MOWBRAY MARRAS.

Chorus.

MRS. CAMPBELL PERUGINI, MRS. BLAIR LEIGHTON, MISS CHRISTINE CONNELL, MISS JANET CONNELL, MR. MOWBRAY MARRAS, MR. W. HERBERT ROE, MR. WILLIAM ALLEN, MR. T. HAMILTON JACKSON.

———————

CHORUSES and INCIDENTAL MUSIC by MR. B. LUARD-SELBY.

THE DANCES arranged by MISS LILY LINFIELD.

STAGE MANAGER . . . MR. ALFRED LYS BALDRY.

Date of first performance, Monday, May 5th, 1890.

PROLOGUE.

IF the pale shade of old Theocritus,
    Wandered from far Elysium, look on us
With sad yet kindly smile, some genial ray
Of olden sunshine, from the unwithered bay
Crowning his brows, upon our pastoral stage
Fall slantingly and bright, 'tis all our age
Dare hope. Yet, though in sweet Sicilian air,
Which but to breathe were cordial to all care,
We walk not, his impassioned nightingale
Visits us still, with the old rapturous tale
Among our blossoming apple-trees by night,
Shy and yet constant. So, not banished quite
By Babel and its din, where once she set
Her buskined feet in triumph, lingers yet
The shy Muse in that Thespian bower she ranged
Singing, ere yet the speech of man was changed
For tones unrhythmical. O, let none sneer
If, singing still, she strive to charm your ear
With vowelled verse, to set before your eyes
An Idyll, picturing 'neath sunnier skies
The shepherd folk of some dim age of gold,
Which yet the laurelled bards in days of old
Ne'er sang: another age, another art.
And haply even the tir'd modern heart
Still keeps its quiet pastoral places, where
The shy Muse comes. O let us enter there,
There sing, there dance, there act our comedy,
And your good-will amend our poesy !

A SICILIAN IDYLL.

SCENE I.

THE SHEPHERDS' DANCING-PLACE.

A circular space with marble mosaic pavement, skirted by a laurel thicket, and partly shaded by a pergola supported on pillars running diagonally across the stage. At the back of the stage (R. C.), in an alcove at the end of the pergola, stands a terminal statue of Dionysus, crowned with vine-leaves and ripe grapes. The tall pedestal is wreathed with ivy, and around it in the alcove are disposed thyrsi and shepherds' crooks.

Through the pergola is seen a spur of Ætna, with olive-woods and meadows sloping down to the sea.

About half-way up the stage (L.) a marble seat runs around a small segment of the circular pavement, following its curve; and over the back of this seat appears the distant sea, deep blue in the afternoon light. A smaller seat is placed at the foot of one of the pillars (R.), near the front of the stage.

Enter DAPHNIS *playing on his pipe. He breaks off abruptly and sits down on the smaller seat* (R.).

DAPHNIS.

SAD sounds my pipe, sad as the sighing breath
  Voiced by its reed. [*He lets the pipe fall.*] O cruel
    Amaryllis!
For thee my flocks, wanting their shepherd's care,

Stray in the glens ; for thee the wandering bleat
Of the lost lamb but calls some pitiless foe
To still his tender plaint ; for thee their shepherd
Strays, like the shade of an unburied man,
Around the happy haunts of pastoral mirth :
Wander, my flocks, your shepherd is astray!

Enter THESTYLIS *from the back.   She remains in the background
leaning against the curved marble seat.*

THES. Here, where his voice once led the gleeful choir,
Our drooping Daphnis comes to make his moan !

DAPH. Ah, well-a-day ! maker of mirth no more,
I shun the herdsmen's revels, hear far off
Songs of that realm I enter now no more :
Wander, my flocks, your shepherd is astray !
Feel from afar the dance thrill my slow feet,
Which to the Muse's measure beat no more :
Wander, my flocks, your shepherd is astray !

THES. [*Aside.*] Poor Daphnis! thy sad looks infect my
heart,
Which mocked at love, with pity for thy plight.   [*He sighs.*]
Ah, what a sigh was there ! And here I stay
To catch the trick of sighing as I hear.

DAPH. [*Rising, and pacing up and down.*] What boots it though
my pipe charm on the boughs
The silence of an hundred nightingales ?
It charms not Amaryllis ; though my song
Tame with sad sounds the fierce-eyed lynx, or move
The gaunt and cub-drawn wolf in very ruth
To spare the trembling kid between her paws ?
It moves not Amaryllis.   Wander still,

My flocks forlorn; for Daphnis never more
Shall pasture you 'mid gleaming dews of morn :
Stray, my sheep, for your shepherd is astray.
Lead you at noon by shady streams, or ope,
When Hesper lights his lamp, your fencéd fold :
Stray, my sheep, for your shepherd is astray.

THES. [*Aside.*] No mateless bird, forsaken on the bough,
Made ever more melodious threnody.

DAPH. Farewell, my half-grown lambs, and ewes new-shorn,
Whose wealthy fleeces were my pride ; farewell
My soft-eyed cows, from whose deep udders flow
Rivers of milk ! No more I'll plead for love
With unpersuasive breath.

THES. [*Aside.*]   Wisely resolved.
But whither from these valleys will he flee ?

DAPH. There is a marsh my browsing goats have found
Where the gaunt hemlock's pipy stems grow rank
With lurid speckles, in whose clammy cells
Lurks death's oblivious wine. This will I drink,
And lay me down by Amaryllis' door,—
With the scorned singer's life end all my songs.

THES. [*Aside.*] O 'tis a fool ! And yet a sweet-voiced fool !
Did he woo me, I too might play the fool,
And Eros, god of fools, have double praise. [*She comes forward.*
Thou, Daphnis, here, preluding with fond words
Deeds fonder yet ?

DAPH.   Forbear me, Thestylis !
Thou art the cold companion of the scorn
That ices my swift blood. Mock me not now ! [*Is about to go.*

THES. Stay, Daphnis ; for I bring thee ruth, not scorn.
Lift, shepherd, lift thy heavy-lidded eyes,

Dull with long vigils of unhappy love.
Mad lover, wilt thou carry thy sweet songs
To Hades, and untimely rob the world
And leave thy lovers mourning?   *[She takes up his pipe.*
                Take again
Thy flute of sweetest stop.   Play, sing, and live.
                      [He turns away.
    Daph. Hope shuns me: I am out of love with life.
    Thes. All things that live may hope; the dead alone
Stare from the sullen gloom with hopeless eyes.
Come, sing no more to savage brakes and fells,
Or that more savage still, a loveless heart;
But sing to me, and glut my passionate ear
With music of thy passion: sing to me!   *[Offering the pipe.*
    Daph. *[Taking it.]* Can the dead sing? I am a fleeting ghost,
An alien in the sun of human joy.
And thou, her comrade, whose disdain's cold air
I breathe and die in, O what recks thy heart
Of love?   Wherefore begone and mock me not!
              [Places the pipe in his belt, and turns away.
    Thes. Sad shepherd, I am pity, not disdain,
And come to crave the pity that I yield,   *[She sighs.*
Being fallen into thy case.
    Daph. *[Turning to her.]* Most wretched maid!
    Thes. Eros, the potent god, hath quelled my spirit
With one swift bolt.   Daphnis, I love, I love—
A youth, Daphnis, a youth who loves not me.
             [They move up the stage towards the seat.
    Daph. Can love's soft dews bedim the shining morn,
Thestylis, of those eyes?   Women can weep
False tears, I know, with laughter on their lips:

Yet wilt thou play with me, I'll play a while
For very luxury of woe, with thee.

THES. [*Sitting.*] O, could I sing like thee, solace my woe
With lovely words that kiss each other quick
In dancing rhymes, forsooth I would not die !

DAPH. Alas ! to sing is to redouble pain ;
For when I make sweet songs of happy love,
How passionate Cynthia through the ambrosial dusk
Of the scarce-whispering laurels, in sweet shame,
Stole to her Latmian shepherd, I grow faint
With imaged blisses mocking empty arms.
O Tantalus, o'er-pitied Tantalus,
Thy torments are but the shadows of the state
Of him who loves unloved !

THES. A silver tongue,
Daphnis, thou givest my hidden bitter wound.
O love !—I knew not what an ancient woe
Lived in that word, till now I hear thee speak.

DAPH. O flee my tongue, whose plaint infects the wind
With its own sadness, and attunes the voice
Of every wandering echo in the woods
To sighing falls ; ay, every rock and tree,
The birds, the streams, the melancholy glades
Most loved of brooding Pan, I have taught them all
To utter but one word, whose venomed sweetness
Is death to hear : Love, Love ! But her disdain
Looks from the eyes of heaven, whence all night long
Ten thousand flames of virgin cruelty
Flash scorn on love and me.

THES. [*Rising, and laying her hand on his shoulder.*] Come,
    Daphnis, come !

We two lost creatures, let us to the wilds ;
With murmured songs and sad antiphonics,
There let us court oblivion.   Come away !

DAPH.   The Hyblan bees, flying from Ætna's flank,
Crawl drunken from the luscious ivy-flowers,
O'er-surfeited with sweets ; and, richly fed,
Die of their ecstasy : I starve on sighs.
Oh, I must herd with all despisèd things,
With all defeated things, despairing things ;
A drone, thrust from the comfortable hive
To dream of honey-drops, die of the sting !

THES.   Nay, Daphnis, lift thy head in manly pride,
Tears are for women's eyes ; with plaints of woe
Was never woman won.   Come, in sad sport
Call me thy Amaryllis, woo me so ;
I'll teach thee how to woo, and win thy suit.

DAPH.   I'll call thee death, and woo thee then indeed,
With all love's sweetest, most endearing names. [*Music heard.*
But hark ! I hear the hated sound of mirth !
Here to their dancing-place the shepherds come,
With pipe and throbbing tabor.   Hence, away !

[*Exit by upper entrance,* L.

THES.   Now, Daphnis, thou shalt gaze into mine eyes,
See thine own image there, and learn to love
The flattering mirror that doth image thee. [*Exit, following him.*

Enter (R.) *Chorus of* YOUTHS *and* MAIDENS, *crowned with ivy,
   and with thyrsi in their hands, and led by a* PRIEST OF BACCHUS,
   *bearing an amphora of new wine.   They sing a hymn to Bacchus,
   moving rhythmically over the stage.*

A SICILIAN IDYLL.

HYMN TO BACCHUS.
Strophe.

O thou, renowned by many a mystic name,
Lord of the vintage, Bacchus, who dost cheer
With glory of the grape the sun-burnt year,
With wine the heart of labour—wine whose flame,
Stol'n from the sun for man's delight,
Crowns winter's cup with golden summer's grace !
God of the flaming face,
We hail thee, genial god ! Come to us now
With festal footsteps o'er the glowing earth,
And purple clusters nodding round thy brow,
Welcomed with every seasonable rite,
Dances, and pastoral mirth !

Antistrophe.

But come not, as to those who love thee not,
Thy panther Mœnads with their panther kin
Furiously leaping to the frantic din
Of clashing cymbals, their flush'd faces hot,
Smear'd from limbs torn in the glare
Of blazing torches reeling through the smoke !
Come, worshipt of our folk,
Lord of the mellowing year ! Come, for we come
With ankles splash'd with vintage, honouring thee
With must from foaming vats ; bless now thy home,
Dear as grey Thebes, or Nysa of sweet air,
Thy own laughing Sicily !

VINTAGE DANCE.

Then enter AMARYLLIS (L.), *a wine-cup in her hand.   They salute
her, and the* PRIEST *pours wine from the amphora into her cup.*

AMARYL. Now to the bounteous god, whose opulent hand
Is potent on our vineyards and our vines,
Honour be given ! [*She makes a libation.*] Hail, jocund vintagers !
I bid you to our customary feast.
Wide, for your welcome, open stand my doors,
Swept is the threshing-floor, my damsels wait
By tables ranged and ready.   Welcome all !

1ST SHEP. Thanks, Amaryllis, whom all gods conspire
To bless with all the wealth our peasants prize,
And beauty more desired than flocks and herds.

ALL. Bacchus !   Hail, Bacchus !   On to the vintage feast !
[AMARYLLIS *seats herself on the upper seat.*
Exeunt Chorus, L.

Enter THESTYLIS *behind.   She bends over the seat and kisses*
AMARYLLIS.

AMARYL. Where, Thestylis, have strayed thy truant feet
These three long days ?

THES. [*Sits beside* AMARYLLIS.] Something I am to blame ;
Yet, most dear Amaryllis, chide me not.

AMARYL. But wherefore in good sooth growest thou so
strange ?
Hast thou a sorrow, and not share with me ?
A joy not halved with me and doubled so ?

THES. Believe me, I am still thy constant friend.

AMARYL. Still, Thestylis ?   That still sounds ominously !
Hast thou not been the sister of my choice,
Dearer than one born of my father's blood ;
Of more immortal kinship ?

THES.   That I am.

AMARYL. Have we not, friendship's twins, with linkèd arms
Walked in one way, content?   Have we not vowed
Our souls in maiden wedlock to each other,
And railed at love, the enemy of our vows!

THES. Ay, we have railed at love.   But, Amaryllis——

AMARYL. What! has that subtle foe with flattering guile
Won thy fond worship?   Am I left alone?

THES. I would but plead for one who loves thee well.
I have seen Daphnis, but so woe-begone,
So pale with poring long on passion's book,
So out of love with life, I could not choose
But pity him.   Thyself hadst pitied him.

AMARYL. [*Rising impatiently and crossing*, R.]   These are the
      tricks of men, to win the tears
Of silly girls.

THES. [*Following her.*] What if the man should die
For love of thee?   For so, by every oath
Our love-lorn shepherds use, he swears he will.

AMARYL. Now by our own true love thou angerest me
With such swift dotage!   Daphnis die of love!
Ay, a fair death in words ; and yet live on
To see maids weeping o'er his epitaph.
For love of me or thee, or any woman,
Never went man to sleep under the clods
His transient pain away.   The fabled swan
Dies singing, the crost lover loves again.

THES. It is a foolish fashion of our vales
That men whom love ne'er slew foredo themselves,
Thinking they die of love.   So Battus gave
His bright head to the keeping of the sea,

When Gorgo had undone him with her scorn.

AMARYL. Fear not for Daphnis. Sick self-love, that makes
With fond conceit many a tall shepherd pale,
Hath set the stripling pining for a dream.

THES. For dreams men die. It is a world of dreams.
We clothe ourselves in dreams, we clothe in dreams
The naked limbs of life that we may live
Unscathed of the dread vision ; and the glimpse
'Twixt fading dream and dream is dangerous to us.
For Daphnis, in that perilous pass, I fear.
The sickness he had caught from thy cold eyes
Sits heavy on him now. The man will die.

AMARYL. [*Crossing*, L.] Give him fair burial then, in thine
        own arms,
For thou art dead, the Thestylis I knew,
And I must weep for thee. [*Sitting, and turning to Thestylis*] O
        Thestylis,
How I have loved thee ! Thy sweet looks, thy words,
Thy tones live in me still. Thy little gifts,
Small dainty things thy hands in secret wrought
For tokens of thy love, I have kept them all.

THES. As I keep thine.   [*Approaches her.*
AMARYL.   And now, like summer's birds,
They will come no more. O, what a secret glee
Made vivid every sense when I could think
My thoughts would soon wed thine ! My murmuring heart
In absence ever kept sweet dialogue
With thine. And now, O, now, that music's done! [*Turns away.*
    THES. [*Kneeling and clasping* AMARYLLIS.] Gusts of a more
        imperious music now
Thrill me, as song-birds thrill the April woods ;

A thousand sad sweet thoughts are vocal in me,
And long to sing their secrets in thine ear.

    AMARYL. [*Rising.*] Better go cast thy limbs into the fire,
Or dungeon up thy body from the sun,
Than scorch thy being in love's bitter flame !
            [*Crosses, L., and comes down the stage.*

    THES. I cannot tell. My mother loved a man :
I fear I am her daughter.

    AMARYL.   I have seen
The tedious tragedies of woman's life
No poet's tongue dare sing, too mean, too common
To tread the scene in pomp of tragic words ;
The sullen agonies, the ageing cares,
The dull disease whereof poor famished love
Dies dumbly hour by hour a lingering death.

    THES. [*Approaching.*] But wherefore should love die, folding
       his wings
Among the household gods, whose homely forms
Catch splendour from the rapture of his face ?

    AMARYL. Alas ! if love were all that women dream,
His were a name worth worship ; and the light
Of his stern face would so renew the world,
The race of man would grow divine as he ;
For we are priestesses of that pure flame
Whose temple is the soul ; but our dull shepherds
Honour a power unknown with wanton rites
And gross initiations, clowns unschooled,
Who serve their uncouth image of the god,
But not the god indeed.

    THES.   Thou, Amaryllis,
Hast ever roamed the mind's high mountain-peaks,

Lone shepherdess of thought's wide-wandering flocks.
I am the creature of a lowlier sphere,
And love the broken colours of this earth,
Its trivial joys, its very household cares
That move thy spleen.   My hand upon the loom
Sets my heart singing to the busy purr
Of the swift shuttle.   Heaven's bright waggoner,
Who trots his punctual round with pleasant face,
Tasking and toiling, claims me of his school.
For day by day he comes with jovial cheer,
Comforts man's lot, and ripes his corn, and swells
His grapes with delicate juice : so, in his sight,
Run I my daily round of cheerful toil.
I fear I am in love with dull content ;
My very dreams are woven of common things.

    AMARYL. Nay, thou art worthier far than I ! the bright
Creative word of love is potent in thee,
Thy daily tasks are ministries of love.
I am the brooding sorrow of this earth,
Pining for things to come.   But, Thestylis,
I grudge thee, with more desperate jealousy
Than a mere sister's, for I love thee. more,
To any sighing shepherd of them all.

    THES. Must the poor shepherd lack his shepherdess ?
Methinks the power that shaped us man and maid
Moves us to dance in couples, not alone.

    AMARYL. Ay, were the bonds but equal, mate with mate,
Twin-yoked in love ! But all the world's awry.
War in our souls, our very loves are wars
Where one alone keeps treaty.   When a man
Sits like a conqueror in a captive town,

No more sweet words, no kind observances—
Ah! Thestylis, wilt thou wed a swarm of cares,
Slave for a thankless lord, nurse crying babes
Who, like ungrateful nestlings, quit the nest
And leave it cold, because a shepherd sighs?
                              [*Moves up the stage and sits.*

THES. A grain of love savours a peck of cares.
                    [*Follows, and leans over the back of the seat.*
But, tell me, Amaryllis, hast thou never
Caught thy heart sighing for a love beyond
The friendship of a girl?

AMARYL.   I would not change it
For the contemptuous lordship of a fool.

THES. Nor I, in sooth.

AMARYL.   But——

THES.   Well?

AMARYL.   If I did love,
I should be dangerous to the man I loved.
No more of these vain dreams : I thank the gods
I love no man!

THES. [*Coming round the seat and crossing to* L.] No man is
      worth thy love,
Since heroes come no more.   But now farewell!
I must go seek my sighing counterpart.
When our great baby, man, cries for the moon,
We must e'en comfort him.

AMARYL.   Provide him then
Corals to cut his wisdom-teeth upon,
Or much I fear the babe will bite his nurse.

THES. Corals or none, the babe will bite his nurse.

AMARYL. Farewell!

D

THES.   Farewell, sweet sister of my soul:
Despise me not too much, and love me still.

                                    [*Exit* THESTYLIS, L.

AMARYL. [*Gazing after her.*] Is friendship too a dream?
    this wingless love
I have templed in my breast, can he fly too?
I am grown old in loving, and my heart,
Blank as a house where lies the master dead,
Crowned with pale funeral flowers, looks on a world
Grown suddenly grey.   Who shall inhabit now
The emptied chambers?   What shall ever break
Its dismal peace, where not a sound of life
Flutters the ordered silence of its halls?   [*She remains musing.*

        Enter (R.) ALCANDER.   *He comes near her unperceived.*

ALCAN. [*Aside.*] This should be that disdainful shepherdess
I come to woo.   Now boldness be my speed!
[*Aloud.*] Pardon, fair maiden, that with tongue too rude
I break your reverie.

AMARYL.   Who speaks?

ALCAN.   A man.

AMARYL. 'Tis a brave title.   [*She looks gravely at him.*

ALCAN.   An amazing one?

AMARYL. Not so.   The title truly is not rare.

ALCAN. No, nor methinks the thing it signifies.

AMARYL. [*Rising and coming down the stage,* L.] Well, I have
    seen many a tall bearded shape
That called itself a man, was not a woman,
And went erect upon two legs like man,
And yet——

ALCAN. Yet?——

AMARYL. Lacked erectness of the mind.
The soul, methought, like some dull grazing beast,
Looked ever on the ground.

ALCAN. They were in love.
Went they not so? [*Paces to and fro.*] With such head-hanging
sighs?
Their arms crost thus? Some woman was the cause.

AMARYL. Some woman?

ALCAN. Ay. Are we not women's sons,
And made or marred by women? For this love
'Tis a most foolish passion.

AMARYL. Have you felt it,
That you deride it so?

ALCAN. Well, ay, and no.
I am too much in love to keep in love
With any woman I have ever seen.
Unseen I love them all, most constantly.

AMARYL. What lacked they then, the women you have
seen?

ALCAN. Nothing, but that which, lacking, they lacked all:
The power that draws, as the moon draws the waves,
The tides of manhood to their highest flood;
That kindles soul and sense into one flame;
That rouses, and assuages, and sustains
The spirit of passion in us, till to love
Mates us with heroes. Lacking this, anon
They set me yawning. [*Sits on smaller seat*, R.] Ye gods,
breathes there no woman
To drain the aching homage of my heart!

AMARYL. [*Aside.*] Here is a man in jest speaks mysteries.
[*Aloud.*] 'Tis with yourself then that you are in love.

Have you not spied in some clear mountain pool
Your sun-crowned image and adored it straight?

ALCAN. [*Springing up and moving towards her.*] Not so, by
    Heracles! I am too much
A man to love the image of a man!
I love an unseen woman ; but am come
Into these valleys to be cured of love.

AMARYL. How cured?

ALCAN.   E'en by the sight of her.

AMARYL.   You seem
A most strange lover.

ALCAN.   A most ardent one.
I have sought her, dark or fair, an hundred times,
Called her in secret by an hundred names,
Each the fair label of a bride so fair
She baffled poor conceiving ; but when I came
In sight of her, lo! the shy nymph was gone,
And in her place a pitiful siren smiled.

AMARYL. Haply you knew her not, though there she
    stood.
'Twas but some imperfection in the eye
Through which you looked, no true defect in her.

ALCAN. Ay, some imperfect blindness, very like ;
For love, they say, is blind. It may be so.

AMARYL. Then are you no true lover. But you yourself,
Are you so rich in graces, built so high
In all perfections, that you cannot stoop
To match save with perfection?

ALCAN. Oh, for me,
I count myself neither the first of men,'
Nor yet the meanest—all the more a man :

Most precious to myself, and, being framed
Of infinite desires, resolved to reign
King of the world I conquer.   Wherefore then
Should I content myself but with the best ?

AMARYL. [*Approaching him.*] You speak not like a shepherd
    of these vales,
And wear the Phrygian bonnet, as I see.
Come you from far ?

ALCAN.   Out of the fires of Troy,
Whose siege blind Homer sang.

AMARYL.   O wonderful !
So many centuries old, and not yet grey ?

ALCAN. My stock I mean.   Alcander is my name,
Evander's son.   Yonder my mountain home.

AMARYL. Are you then that Alcander, who bore off
So many prizes from the harvest games,
Our wondering shepherds vowed that Heracles
Was come again in you ?

ALCAN.   No Heracles
I boast myself, but surely that Alcander.

AMARYL. You have done great things.

ALCAN.   A unit in the van
Of many ciphers may look monstrous big,
Yet in itself be but a cipher still.

AMARYL. Nay, you o'erthrew stout Ægon, and out-ran
Wing-footed Corydon, best of their time.
But, for this nymph you seek, in what fair name
Has the hoarse beldame Rumour crooned to you
The inventory of her charms ?

ALCAN.   To find her home,
For somewhere here she dwells, did I accost you.

Her name is Amaryllis, and her sire
Damætus left her late vineyards and farms,
And wealth in flocks and herds ; but let them be ;
For me, I set no store by sheep and goats,
Or such base cattle, while a woman's by.

AMARYL. How, then, speaks Rumour of this new unseen
Perfection that you follow?

ALCAN.   Very ill.
She is proclaimed a shrew ; but beautiful,
Cruel to men, they say ; but beautiful,
Colder than mountain snows ; but beautiful
To abash the tongue of praise ! therefore I love her.
A most unnatural maid, she hates all men,
Therefore I love her ! Nature, moulding her,
Disdained her common patterns ; therefore I love her.

AMARYL. You praise her very strangely.

ALCAN.   By report.

AMARYL. And you have sought her to be cured of love?

ALCAN. Ay, I have been too long love's fool, and now
I come to see her, and be cured of love.

AMARYL. See, and be cured then : I am Amaryllis.

ALCAN. Alas, how Rumour lies ! [*Sits on seat* (R.) *and gazes
at her.*] They said your skin
Was whiter far than snow, redder your lips
Than coral just o'erwhispered by the surge,
Your hair more lustrous than the noonday sun,
Your voice the nightingale's, your eyes twin stars,
Each bright as Sirius when Orion soars
With pendant feet above the southern wave ;
If so, I am gone blind.

AMARYL.   Nay, you have seen,

And so are cured.   [*She turns away.*

ALCAN. [*Rising and approaching.*] Oh, by no means! My cure
Is not so light a thing. Think you I came
To clasp a bride of snow, to vex my lips
With kissing coral, or to fret mine eyes
With staring on the noonday sun? Not so;
I came to find a woman such as you,
No more, no less, and in her eyes my fate.

AMARYL. You are the strangest wooer I have known.
Pity you come so far to seek your fate:
You must go bootless home.

ALCAN.   Ay, it were pity
I should go bootless home. But I trust well
I shall not. Having seen you, I have found
The one worth winning. And you, do you not feel
The deeps within you rise in sudden flood
At the calling of your fate?

AMARYL.   No.

ALCAN.   But you shall,
Or Rumour spoke one truth: you have no heart.

AMARYL. Perhaps I have no heart.
           [*Moves up towards the upper seat.*

ALCAN.   Put it to proof;
Give me—you will?—before we part, one kiss.

AMARYL. Shepherd, you grow too bold!
           [*Retires up the stage towards the alcove.*

ALCAN. [*Leaning against the seat.*]   I would dare all
To win you, and will dare. There is an old
Rough wooer's custom in our mountain glens,
That he who woos must strive for a first kiss;
'Twill serve me here.   [*He approaches her.*

AMARYL. [*Rushing towards front of stage.*] Back, madman!

ALCAN. [*Grasping her arm.*] Love is mad.

    [*He clasps her in his arms. They struggle. He kisses her.*
You have fought well, but I rest conqueror.

                        [*She bursts his hold.*

AMARYL. Rough clown, begone!

ALCAN.   Oh, fairest, pardon me!
Never again will I demand from you
Save what you freely give.

    AMARYL. [*Half-drawing her dagger.*] If I should kill you!

    ALCAN. You will not. That imperious heart of yours
I felt but now bounding beneath my hand
Will plead for me. As well hold back the sun
From rising, or keep out the leaping tide,
Or stay the operation of the winds,
As bar out love, come at his destined hour.

    AMARYL. Begone!   [*Sheathes dagger.*

    ALCAN.   I will begone, till you recall me.

                        [*Retiring,* R.
I am your fate, remember, and you mine. [*Exit* ALCANDER, R.

    AMARYL. [*Pacing restlessly.*] I have drunk the wine of Circe,
        and my sense
Reels in some hateful change. The mirroring brook
As I pass by, will shew me a changed face:
I am no more myself. What hath he seen
In me: what base connivance of my soul,
That he should dare this outrage? Still I feel
The power of his bold eyes, still bear about me
His arms' captivity! Oh, to be free
From these tyrannic moments that bear chains
To clank long years upon the limbs of life

And shame the careless past! This place of mirth
Grows dreadful, and the vines tangling the boughs
Seem webs on the dark loom of weaving fate.
My thoughts grow mad!

END OF SCENE I.

SCENE II.

THE SHEPHERD'S DANCING-PLACE. NIGHT.

THESTYLIS *discovered seated on the smaller seat* (R.), ALCANDER
standing by her.

THESTYLIS.

YOU have done more than all our shepherds could.
    ALCAN. Why, what brave deed is that?
  THES.   Have you not won
A kiss from Amaryllis?
  ALCAN.   I take shame
It was so rudely won. Oh, had you seen her,
The lightning in her eyes, her cheeks aflame
With sudden anger, then so sternly pale;
Her lips, more gracious than the lily's flower
In their proud sculpture, curved in scorn; and I
The clownish wind, rough spoiler of her sweets,
That shook that splendid lily! I could have knelt
And kist her virgin feet, and sued for pardon.

E

How she must hate me!

THES.   Ay, but of such hate
May love be born.   Trust me, she thinks of you.
You have made fever in her days and nights,
Filled her with visions, shaken her with strange thoughts.
Two days and nights she is a vexèd sea,
Restless and moody as the wild-eyed herds
When Pan afflicts.   What wonder if she hate you?

ALCAN. Even such a trouble hath she sown in me.
Were I a man of words, I could become
A sigher like the rest, and hang my head,
Making of her sweet name a thousand songs.

THES. If songs could win her, every sighing swain
Had had his part of her, ere you came by.

ALCAN. Well, by the gods, I have no trick of song,
And love no other music than her name.
O divine Amaryllis! O barren phrase
To sound the wordless worship of my soul!
My manhood, matched with her perfection, seems
A graceless churl, with sacrilegious hand
Making assault upon the golden doors
Of Cynthia's temple, till the victory
I dreamed of looks a crime.

THES.   Be not cast down;
So love conspire to give you victory,
She will forgive her victor.

ALCAN.   O that fate
Would set a hundred heroes in her view
And bid me match them all, though each exploit
Cost me a death achieving! Each proud drop,
Warm from my breast, would laugh to kiss her feet,

Uttering Alcander's love.   Might she not give me
For guerdon, ere I died, one gracious smile ?
 THES. Why, that were more than singing.   But keep your
  blood ;
You shall have better comfort than a smile
To light you Charon's way.   One living lover
Were, for my choosing, worth a dozen dead.

  Enter DAPHNIS, L.   *He remains at the side, half-hidden by a
     laurel-bush.*

 THES. [*Aside.*] Now god of jealousy, arm the god of love,
And we shall play the daintiest comedy !
 ALCAN. You give me hope then ?

    Enter from the back AMARYLLIS.

THES.   Kiss my hand upon it.
          [*He kisses her hand.*

 DAPH. [*Aside.*] What man is this ?   O Thestylis, I see
Thou art become the general comforter !
 THES. [*To* ALCANDER.] Here comes my lover with his heart
  in twain,
Help me to make it whole.   Come, woo me, woo me !
 ALCAN. [*Taking her hands.*] I have twin kids, fairest of that
  fair breed
That makes my father's wealth : these with their dam
I'll give thee ; and a bowl of sycamore
Well-carved and waxed, and virgin to the lip,
So thou but look with favour on my suit.
 DAPH. [*Aside.*] O veering mind of woman !   Shall I speak ?
 THES. Go, fetch thy offering : words are empty breath.
         [*Exit* ALCANDER, R.
 AMARYL. [*Aside.*] O now I see that I have been the sport

Of this most common wooer! Swift to my vengeance,
Before this insult grows a shepherd's tale !

[*Exit* AMARYLLIS *at the back of the stage*, L.

THES. [*Aside.*] Love in her heart and hatred on her brows
Speeds Amaryllis like a summer storm.
And now for Daphnis. [*To* DAPHNIS.] Ha! what man art thou ?
Alcander ?

DAPH.   Daphnis ! O false Thestylis !
Sink not thy lids for shame to look on me ?

THES. Wherefore ?   To look upon an eaves-dropper ?
But thou wilt keep my counsel, gentle youth ?

DAPH. I'll to the wilds and live a savage man,
For there's no truth in woman.

THES.   What is this ?

DAPH. Thy kindness is as fickle as the sea,
Vain as the solace of a flattering wind
That sets the ship singing upon her course,
Then strikes anon the shuddering sail aback.

THES. O man's ingratitude !

DAPH.   Didst thou not swear
A thousand pretty oaths to be my friend,
To follow me through the world, make me once more
In love with glosing life ?   Yet now, forsooth——

THES. You deem yourself a master with his maid.
May I not hear a wooer ?   Have I not
Plodded your errands, pleaded your lost cause
With Amaryllis, angered her with my tears,
Made rash divorce in very flowering-time
Between the close-twined branches of our love,
To gain but gloomy looks, cross words from you ?

DAPH. Mock me no more with the forgotten tune

Of Amaryllis' name.   O Thestylis,
Thou knowest full well with what a conquering charm
Of gentle tones and looks thou hast beguiled me.
Why came thy face haunting the dusk of dreams,
Where Amaryllis, like a setting star,
Sank out of seeing?   All my love for her
Seems but the memory of a crocus-flower,
Whose transient flame in cold unbudded woods
Heralds the coming spring, to one imbathed
In blithe and glowing air, when golden May
Peoples with summer lilies plain and hill.

    THES. Sits the wind so?   And have I won the prize
Of thy inconstant heart?

    DAPH.   Inconstant?   Ay,
As the unresting flower that seeks her god
With ever-roaming gaze.   So, constant still
To love, I turn from an outwearied hope
To find the very substance of that hope.

    THES. You turn from fickle thoughts to flattering words.

    DAPH. If I have doted on the alien stars
In the absence of the sun, 'twas but the dim
Fore-feeling of the worship I should render
His genial presence when he rose indeed.
And, Thestylis, I thought the sun was up,
And all his comfort shining in thine eyes.
I was deceived.   Farewell, live happily!
I'll to the untrodden glades, where brooding Pan
Pipes to his unkind love, shepherd the clouds
Of fantasy, and tame with sad sweet song
The satyr's uncouth tribes.

    THES.   Stay, Daphnis, stay!

Daph. I'll live no more the mirth of laughing girls.

[Exit, R.

Thes. Nay, thou shalt find me clinging as the burr
Caught in the tangles of the curling fleece.

[Exit, following him.

Enter Amaryllis with an Attendant carrying a tripod with a
brazier of burning coals.

Amaryl. Set it down here. Give me the magic herbs,
The barley and the wax, and now begone!
Wait on my call.

[Exit the Attendant, L. Amaryllis casts incense on the fire.
Ay, leap, thou flickering flame, avenge me well
On him who hath filled my breast with throbbing fire!

[She begins her incantation, pacing around the tripod.

The Incantation.

Hear me, Selene, for to thee I sing!
Calling on thee by thy most dreadful name,
Hecate; thou who through the shuddering night
Pacest where black pools of fresh-offered blood
Gleam cold beside the barrows of the dead:
Dread goddess, draw him dying to my feet!

Hear me, Selene, for to thee I sing!
The deep moans at thy coming, and the pines
Murmur and shed their pungent balm; scared wolves
Howl in the glens, and dogs, with bristling hair,
Whine as thou standest in the triple way:
Dread Mother, draw him dying to my feet!

Hear me, Selene, for to thee I sing!
Around this bowl I have tied in scarlet wool
Witch-knots against Alcander.   Let him feel
As many pangs in his false heart, who kissed
My lips in mockery and disdains me now:
Dread goddess, draw him dying to my feet!

Hear me, Selene, for to thee I sing!
I cast this barley on the fire, and say :
" Even so I scatter strong Alcander's bones ! "
I fling these laurel-leaves upon the fire,
And say : " So let his flesh be shrivelled up ! "
Dread Mother, draw him dying to my feet!

Hear me, Selene, for to thee I sing !
Lo, as I melt this wax, melt thou his heart,
Alcander's heart——

   [*She breaks her incantation, and remains standing over*
     the tripod, the wax still in her hand.

Alas ! my spells are vain.   Upon myself
My charms take hold.   My flesh burns, and my heart
Is melted in the furious fires of love,
And my hate burns : I love him, yet I know
That now he loves me not, he loves me not!

    [*She moves restlessly over the stage.*

I am no stronger than the common tribe
Of women, whom I scorned when tyrant love
Moved them to piteous deeds—abandonments,
Abasements ; and amazed find in myself
That hungering heart which makes us passion's fools !

  [*She recommences her incantation, pacing around the tripod.*

Hear me, Selene, for to thee I sing!
I love him, I love him, him who loves me not,
And that is shame.　O turn his heart to me,
Or smite him dead, and let me die with him,
And hide me in the grave from my own scorn :
Dread Mother, draw him only to my feet!

>　　　　　　　[*She leans against a pillar*, L. C.

Short symphony.　Then enter ALCANDER (R.) *swooning, borne in by two* SHEPHERDS.　*They lay him upon the marble seat, then salute* AMARYLLIS.

2ND SHEP. Hail, Amaryllis! Alcander bids thee hail!

>　　　　　　　[*Exeunt* SHEPHERDS, R.

AMARYL. What have I done?　[*She stands gazing at* ALCANDER.

>　　　　　　　I knew not what I did.

>　　　　　　　[*She approaches him.*

So soon struck down!　Dead, or in a trance?　Not dead,
Not surely dead.　Alcander, speak to me!
O speak to me!　　　　　　　[*He opens his eyes.*

ALCAN. [*Sternly.*] Look on thy work, enchantress.

AMARYL.　　　　　　　　　　　All amazed
To think it is my work.　O how fare you?

ALCAN. In mercy take thy sorceries from my heart.

AMARYL. I will unweave my spells.

>　　[*She tears the woollen cord from the bowl, and extinguishes the fire in the brazier.*

Mother of charms,
Scatter upon the winds my baleful words,
Defeat their operation on this man,
Or turn upon myself their malison!

[*Calling.*] Praxinoe! [*Enter* ATTENDANT.] Hence with this
    accursed thing.   [*The* ATTENDANT *removes the tripod.*

   ALCAN. [*Recovering.*] For this swift succour, thanks ! I feel
    the touch
Of the cool fingers of delicious ease.
But hast thou taken harm ?   [*He attempts to rise.*

   AMARYL.   Behold I stand
Unscathed !

   ALCAN. [*Sinking back.*] Then let me die, but die for-
    given
Love's reckless wrong.   To thy stern maidenhood
I bring stern expiation : here I lie,
My manhood's pride the strength of a sick babe,
And I, who loved the ardours of life's day
As eagles love the sun, untimely sent
To pace the pallid coasts of Acheron.

   AMARYL. Thou shalt not die. My frantic fury played
With rites unholy, like a petulant child,
When thou didst slight me with a feignèd love.

   ALCAN. [*Half rising.*] A feignèd love ? I loved, and love
    thee still,
As all oaths that ever lover swore
Could never tell thee.

   AMARYL.   Flatteries do me wrong,
I claim the simple courtesy of truth.
Didst thou not woo the laughing Thestylis,
My own false friend, with lover's gifts this night ?

   ALCAN. Thestylis ? I wooed her but in pretty sport,
By swift suggestion of her prankish wit,
To move her amorous Daphnis, who stood by
In jealous ambush, to more jealousy.

AMARYL. [*Aside.*] Daphnis! I had forgot him. [*Aloud.*] Oh,
is this true ?

ALCAN. Yea, by the soul of truth in thine own soul,
And in my heart, whose weak o'ermastered tides
Thou hast made ebb from the fair coasts of life,
As through thy hate I die for love of thee.

AMARYL. Alas! I hate thee not. I strove to hate thee,
And impotently wrestled with some god
I would not know, and dared not name. But now
I would recall those proud insurgent waves
To triumph on the sunniest shores of joy.

ALCAN. Nay, I must die. There is no cordial now
Can raise me up, save one ; so rare a thing
I may not have it, dare not ask—thy love.

AMARYL. I have no pride to lie to thee, and say
I love thee not ; no shame to say I love thee,
Since that is true. I know it now—I love thee!
And thus I prove the virtue of my love !

       [*She kisses him on the forehead. His strength returns.*

ALCAN. Now let the nightingales burst into song,
The stars make sudden day in the clear heaven !
There is more potency in thy sweet lips
Than in a thousand charms. O not thy spells,
Thy incantations and wild sorceries
Were deadly to me, but thy merited hate !
Reach now thy hands, raise me up, draw me back
From the cold sunless regions of the dead.

       [*She extends her hands to him. He takes them and stands up.*

AMARYL. If thou hadst gone indeed that gloomy way
I would have followed thee, as faithfully
As love's clear planet, handmaid of the sun,

Follows her lord beneath the whelming waves.

ALCAN. [*Coming forward*, c.] Now let me drink the odorous
    air of night,
Breathe the soft wind that murmurs from yon pines.
This is the breath of life; the winds of life
Flatter my breast with bliss, the sap of life
Sweeps revelling through my blood, and my strong heart
Laughs like a giant, with an uncouth joy,
To taste the infinite pleasures of this world.

    AMARYL. I am thy murderess; kill me!
                  [*Casts herself at his feet.*

    ALCAN. [*Raising her.*]   Nay, I live
By thee, would raise thee to the measureless height
Of my proud worship, stoop and kiss thy feet;
Thy charms, more potent than Medea's drugs,
Have made my youth twice young.

    AMARYL.   Alas! my arts
Were subtle treacheries against thy life.
I hold my own at ransom.

    ALCAN.   Give me thyself
In perfect free surrender. Come to me!
        [*She moves gravely towards him. He takes
              her in his arms.*

    AMARYL. I think I have surrendered. I am come
To a new wondrous country: yet not new,
Familiar as a child's remembered home.
Have we not met before, and loved before,
Loved through long cycles of some golden age?
But can'st thou love me indeed? Say it once more.
How often have I laughed at lovers' vows,
Yet now, methinks, I could half weep to hear

Some foolish passionate oath of constancy
That lovers swear when they forswear themselves.

    ALCAN. Possess me with such high and passionate thoughts
As now leap forth, teemed from conception's cell,
And make me thine, past power to be forsworn.
I love thee so I will not desecrate
Our love's eternal moment with vain breath,
And the mere profanation of an oath.

    AMARYL. Then swear not, only say—say what thou wilt ;
But let me die when I am no more loved !

    ALCAN. If the fine ecstasy of this rich night
Were centred all in one pulsating star
Of life, love, triumph, I could boast that now
I wear it in my breast. I am filled with thee
As winter's veins with philtres of the spring.

    AMARYL. And I am grown a woman in thine arms,
Where I have found my home. The mystery
Of my transfigured soul holds me with awe,
And strikes a silence through me, as of streams
Hushed by the might of the invading sea.

    ALCAN. 'Tis I who have grown a babbler, I who have won
The noblest woman won by headstrong man
Since Theseus clasped his buskined Amazon.
Greatness is in thy gift, fame in thy smile ;
Oh, make me great, lay thy commands on me !
There must be battles for a man to fight
Beyond the deeds of Heracles, or all
That keeps the laurels green on Theseus' head.

    AMARYL. Can I inspire thee so ? I did not dare
To dream the heroic fires of such a love
Could catch their flame from me ; and I grow faint

In the amazement of so deep a joy.

ALCAN. Be thou perpetual priestess of that flame.
          [*He leads her to the marble seat.   They sit.*
Come, sit: and let the ecstatic nightingale
Speak from the heart of silence to our hearts.

Short symphony.   Then enter THESTYLIS *and* DAPHNIS.

DAPH. So wonderful a night there has not been,
A night so entrancèd with the spirit of love,
Since in the silver silence of the woods
Pale Cynthia woke Endymion with a kiss.
And now, methinks, since that fond hour she keeps
Her tenderest benison for all lovers true.

THES. Ay, and to-night love hath changed bows with her,
Or slyly filled her quiver from his own.
Look, Daphnis, where our cruel Shepherdess
Belies her fame!   Art thou not jealous now?

DAPH. Ay, Thestylis, of every coaxing wind
That whispers in thy hair, kisses thy cheek.
But thou shouldst here be jealous; for this man,
Thy last-won lover, looks another way.
Where are those kids, tribute of thy bright eyes,
He promised thee but now?   Come, thou wert best
Content thyself with my wide-feeding flocks,
Shepherd their shepherd; or, in maiden spite,
Go live as lonely as yon maiden moon.

THES. A fair choice truly!   Well, when through the gap
Goes one wise sheep the flock will follow sure.
Come, Daphnis, I must be content with thee.

DAPH. [*Embracing her.*] Be our content a sea, so wide and
     deep,

That we shall ne'er sail o'er, but halcyon-like
Upon its bosom build our floating nest.

THES. 'Tis a blithe night for the young archer god!
Four daintier quarries he hath never struck
Plump with his golden shaft. O liberty,
Dear maiden liberty, must I so soon
Forego thy sweets! And now for Amaryllis;
Haply she hath forgot her chiding mood.

                             [She approaches AMARYLLIS.

Mark, Amaryllis, what a noble friend
Thou hast in me, who freely pardon thee
Though thou hast broken all our friendship's vows,
And stolen my lover!

    AMARYL.   Fair play, Thestylis,
For thou didst first steal mine.

    THES.   A fair exchange;
Or shall we change again? In sooth I care not,
So there be peace between us.

    AMARYL. [*Kissing her.*]   Peace and love!

    ALCAN. Daphnis, I give thee joy.

    DAPH.   As deep a bliss
Be thine, and many days to taste that bliss.

    ALCAN. [*Taking* AMARYLLIS *by the hand and leading her
        forward.*]

Well, I have found the woman that I sought,
Yet am not cured of love. Fair Thestylis,
Thine are the honours of this festal night,
And thou shalt claim thy guerdon from my flocks.

    DAPH. I thank thee in her name, and for thy gift
Thou shalt not lack from me a nuptial song.

    THES. Hail, conquering Eros, thou shalt be the lord

Of all our flocks and herds!

AMARYL.   And hearts and homes.

Enter Chorus of YOUTHS *and* MAIDENS *crowned with myrtle, and with branches of amaranth in their hands. They sing a Hymn to Love, and at the Epode crown the lovers with myrtle and amaranth.*

HYMN TO LOVE.

Strophe.

God of the all-conquering bow,
    First-born yet youngest of all gods,
Eros, for men hymn thee so,
    With amaranth and fair myrtle rods
We come, thy suppliants: myrtle pale
    For love and love's deep ecstasy;
Amaranths, that nor fade nor fail,
    That our loves immortal be!

Epode.

Grant that these thy votaries prove
All the joys, not pangs of love!
With amaranth and myrtle now
Thus we crown them on the brow;
Bring glad Hymen in thy train,
Fold here thy wings, fly not again!

THE END.

CHISWICK PRESS :—C. WHITTINGHAM AND CO., TOOKS COURT,
CHANCERY LANE.

THE BODLEY HEAD, VIGO STREET,
LONDON, W., *October*, 1890.

MR. ELKIN MATHEWS'S
NEW AND FORTHCOMING BOOKS.

Poetical Works.

Imperial 16mo, boards, price 5s. net.

A Sicilian Idyll: a Pastoral Play.
BY JOHN TODHUNTER.

With a Frontispiece by WALTER CRANE.

*Printed on handmade paper at the Chiswick Press, in an edition of 250
copies, at 5s. net, and 50 copies large paper, numbered
and signed, at 10s. 6d. net.*

*** The L. P. copies are nearly all sold.

Foolscap 8vo, buckram, price 6s. net.

Corn and Poppies.
BY COSMO MONKHOUSE.

*Finely printed by R. and R. Clark, of Edinburgh, on handmade paper,
in an edition of 350 copies fcap. 8vo, at 6s. net, and 50 numbered
and signed copies, with proofs of an etching by William
Strang as Frontispiece, crown 4to, large
paper, at 15s. net.*

*** The L. P. copies are all sold

Imperial 16mo, boards, price 5s. net.

Chambers Twain.

BY ERNEST RADFORD.

With a Frontispiece by WALTER CRANE.

Printed on handmade paper at the Chiswick Press, in an edition of 250 copies, imperial 16mo, at 5s. net, and 50 copies numbered and signed, crown 4to, large paper, at 10s. 6d. net.

*** The L. P. copies are nearly all sold.

Royal 16mo, wrapper, price 7s. 6d. net.

Ailes d'Alouette.

BY FRANCIS W. BOURDILLON, M.A.

Choicely printed in Fell's type, on Alton Mills handmade paper, by the Rev. C. H. Daniel, at his Private Press; limited to 100 copies; very few remain.

Crown 4to, wrapper, price 7s. 6d. net.

The Backslider, and other Poems.

BY ANTÆUS [*i.e.* W. J. IBBETT].

Finely printed on handmade paper at the Chiswick Press; limited to 50 copies, of which very few remain.

Crown 4to, half vellum.

The Growth of Love.

BY ROBERT BRIDGES.

Choicely printed in Fell's Old English type on Whatman's handmade paper, by Mr. Daniel, at his Private Press; limited to 100 copies.

Crown 4to, half vellum.

The Feast of Bacchus.

By ROBERT BRIDGES.

*Printed in Fell's Roman type (uniform with foregoing) :
limited to 100 copies.*

16mo, vegetable parchment, price 6s.

Galeazzo : a Venetian Episode ; with other Poems.

By PERCY E. PINKERTON.

With an etched Frontispiece.

*** Only a few remain on sale.

---

*Will shortly be published in booklet form, in two editions,
price 6d. and 1s. net.*

Poor People's Christmas.

By THE HON. RODEN NOEL.

Also, during 1891, *POEMS by the following writers :—*

WALTER CRANE,
F. W. BOURDILLON, M.A.,
THE LATE PHILIP B. MARSTON,
PERCY PINKERTON, ETC.

LONDON: ELKIN MATHEWS, VIGO STREET, W.

Post 8vo, cloth, price 7s. 6d. With an illustration of the Novelist's Châlet, from a pen and ink sketch by his son, Mr. W. M. Meredith, and a Portrait.

George Meredith : Some Characteristics.

By RICHARD LE GALLIENNE.

With a Bibliography by JOHN LANE, and a Note by W. MORTON FULLERTON on the reception of George Meredith's works in America.

** The L. P. edition limited to 75 copies.

Crown 4to, boards, price 10s. 6d. net.

Three Essays : by John Keats.

Now first published in book form, edited with Note by H. BUXTON FORMAN ; finely printed on handmade paper at the Chiswick Press; limited to 50 copies, only a few left.

With a life-mask, taken by HAYDON, as Frontispiece.

SECOND EDITION NOW READY.

Post 8vo, brown buckram, price 7s. 6d.

Robert Browning : Essays and Thoughts.

By JOHN T. NETTLESHIP.

The volume includes the "Essays on Robert Browning's Poetry," published in 1868, which did so much to popularise Mr. Browning's work. The present edition is more than doubled in size, containing additional essays, dealing with poems which have appeared since the publication of the first volume.

75 copies on Whatman large paper ; a few remain.

" When an individual work is dealt with, nothing can be more searching and elaborate than Mr. Nettleship's analysis, and to that analysis those works which have done most to justify the common charge of obscurity have been forced to yield up their meaning. A high and penetrating intelligence was needed for such a task ; and something more than intelligence was needed to make us realise, as Mr. Nettleship has done, the true depth and breadth of the philosophy which underlies the vast and varied body of Browning's poetical work. It is not often that so solid and genuine a piece of thinking is produced in literary criticism."—*Academy.*

Post 8vo, cloth, price 2s.

Dante : Six Sermons.

BY THE REV. PHILIP H. WICKSTEED, M.A.,

Author of " The Alphabet of Economic Science," etc.

These brilliant Lectures form an excellent introduction to the Study of Dante. The original edition, published at 6s. in 1879, has long been out of print and difficult to meet with.

MORE ESSAYS ON DANTE.

Thick 8vo, buckram, price 12s., *with Portrait and Plates.*

Literature and Poetry.

BY PHILIP SCHAFF, D.D. (*St. Andrews*).

Dr. Schaff's Volume consists of Ten Critical Essays upon some of the great Literary Epochs in the World's History. The Articles upon Dante and Dante Literature, English and Foreign, are deeply interesting and valuable. The Titles are : " The English Language," " The Poetry of the Bible," " The Dies Irae," " The Stabat Mater Dolorosa," " The Stabat Mater Speciosa," " St. Bernard as a Hymnist," " The University, Past, Present and Future," " Dante Alighieri," " Poetic Tributes to Dante," and " The Divina Commedia."

Post 8vo, buckram, price 6s.

The Poetry of Tennyson.

By the REV. HENRY VAN DYKE, D.D.

CONTENTS :—Tennyson's First Flight ; The Palace of Art ; Milton and Tennyson ; Two Splendid Failures ; The Idylls of the King ; The Homeric Trilogy, and, The Bible in Tennyson ; Chronological Bibliography of his Works, etc.

Published quarterly, in two editions.

The Pioneer :

A Journal of Literature, Social Progress, Economics, and Ethics.

EDITED BY G. DYKE SMITH.

Two shillings net yearly subscription for ordinary edition.
Four shillings net ditto for special edition on handmade paper.
Postage extra.

Now ready, small 8vo, price Twopence.

Handbook of " The Reading Guild."

Foolscap 8vo, cloth, price 5s.

Letters to Living Artists.

BY PASQUIN JUNIOR.

[*In preparation.*]

Royal 18mo, buckram, price 3s. 6d.

The Student and the Body-Snatcher, and other Trifles.

BY ROBINSON K. LEATHER, M.A., AND RICHARD LE GALLIENNE.

[*Immediately.*]

8vo, wrapper, price 3s. 6d.

Alma Murray, Portrait as Beatrice Cenci.

With critical Notice containing Four Letters from
ROBERT BROWNING.

[*Immediately.*]

8vo, wrapper, price 2s. 6d.

Robert Browning and the Drama.

A Note by W. FAIRFAX.

[*Immediately.*]

*Will be published shortly, medium 8vo, finely printed on handmade
paper, in a limited edition, with Etchings.*

The Story of S. William: The Boy Martyr of Norwich.

From forty contemporary and subsequent Chronicles, all of which are
given in full, with copious Notes and Translations, etc., etc.

By THE REV. FREDERICK WILLIAM ROLFE,

*Late Professor of English Literature and History at S. Marie's College
of Oscott.*

Will be issued shortly, demy 8vo, price 5s. net, in an edition of 150 copies.

Tristan and Isolde.

English words to RICHARD WAGNER'S "Tristan und Isolde," in the
mixed alliterative and rhyming verse of the original.

By ALFRED FORMAN,

Translator of "Der Ring des Nibelungen."

---

*Will be issued shortly, quaintly printed on handmade paper
at the Chiswick Press.*

On the Making and Issuing of Books:

A Brochure addressed to Authors and others.

By C. T. JACOBI, Manager of the Chiswick Press.

ELKIN MATHEWS,
AT THE SIGN OF THE BODLEY HEAD,
VIGO STREET, W.